CONTENTS

WORD FAMILIES

Long and Short *a*

Long and Short *e*

Short *i*

Long and Short *o*

Short *u*

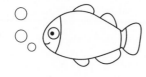

INTRODUCTION

Welcome to *Read, Sort, and Write*. These darling activity books are tons of fun—but they also build essential skills! Every book in the *Read, Sort, and Write* series builds the following skills:

- fine motor (cutting, pasting)
- sorting
- reading
- writing

Read, Sort, and Write: Word Families is a delightful way to teach kids some of the most common word families, using children's natural enjoyment of rhyme and word play to help them become fluent readers.

What are word families? Think of the words *cat*, *rat*, and *mat*. These words both rhyme and end with the same spelling pattern. The fact that their word endings (or phonograms) both sound and look the same means they all belong to the *-at* word family.

SO WHY TEACH WORD FAMILIES?

★ **IT IMPROVES CHILDREN'S DECODING SKILLS ENORMOUSLY.**
Once children learn to read the words *cat*, *rat*, and *mat*, it becomes far easier for them to read words like *slat*, *spat*, *flat*, *that*, and many more. By teaching children to recognize chunks of words, decoding is made far simpler.

★ **IT BOOSTS COMPREHENSION.**
When decoding words becomes easier, children have more mental energy to spend on the ultimate goal of literacy: understanding the words! Children who need to decode, or "sound out," every word in a sentence are likely to have forgotten the first word by the time they get to the last. By then, the meaning has been lost.

★ **IT IMPROVES FLUENCY, SPELLING, AND WRITING.**
The statistics are amazing but true: nearly 500 primary-grade words can be formed from a small group of word families. This means that children not only build sight vocabulary and therefore increase fluency, but also become more familiar with the way words work—making them better spellers and writers, as well!

It's clear that learning word families is essential to reading success. On the other hand, studying and memorizing lists of words is no fun. That's where *Read, Sort, and Write: Word Families* comes in. With this book, kids play with pumpkins, sort fish, and even stack ice cream scoops—all while building the essential skills they need for becoming great readers!

SCHOLASTIC

Read, Sort & Write
WORD FAMILIES

by Pamela Chanko

New York • Toronto • London
Auckland • Sydney • New Delhi • Hong Kong

Cover and interior design by Michelle H. Kim
Images © Scholastic Inc., Shutterstock, The Noun Project

ISBN: 978-1-338-60650-8

Scholastic Inc., 557 Broadway, New York, NY 10012
Copyright © 2020 by Scholastic Inc.
Published by Scholastic Inc.
All rights reserved. Printed in the U.S.A.
First printing, January 2020.

2 3 4 5 6 7 8 9 10   40   26 25 24 23 22 21

HOW TO USE THIS BOOK

THE BASICS

Using the thematic patterns is fun and easy! For every two word families, there are three pages:

1 sorting pieces   **2** sorting mat   **3** writing practice page

Simply copy all three sheets and have kids cut out the pieces. Then have children sort the pieces onto the mat by sorting the words into the correct word families. Afterward, they can practice writing each word on the practice sheet.

FLEXIBLE USES AND FUN VARIATIONS

The activities in this book are designed for maximum flexibility.
Here are just a few tips and ideas:

- Let children color the sorting mat and pieces with crayon. Provide them with lighter shades so the words show through. If children want a permanent piece of artwork, they can glue the pieces down.

- Laminate the mat and pieces for durability. You can keep them in a storage envelope for a puzzle-like sorting activity that kids can do again and again. Keep track of your word family puzzles by labeling the envelopes with the word families they contain.

- The sorting activities and writing practice pages can be set up as an option for center time, or they can be done as seat work. You can also send them home for children to complete with family members, or as homework.

- Have children do the activities independently, or with a partner.

See the following pages for even more ways to customize the activities.

CUSTOMIZATION TOOLS

The thematic patterns in this book contain four words each from 34 of the top word families! Why are they the top word families? Because each family contains so many words! Each word family chosen for this book contains at least twelve words—most have many more—and that's not including proper nouns (such as *Dan* from the *-an* word family or *Spain* from the *-ain* word family).

On pages 7 and 8, you'll find extended word lists for each word family. On pages 61 and 62, you'll find templates for blank cookies and a cookie jar. This way you can focus on additional word families. On pages 63 and 64, you'll find blank sorting pieces for every pattern in this book. This way you can expand each sorting activity to contain more pieces (and more words). You can also differentiate the activities to meet different students' skill levels. Some students may be ready for more sophisticated words, while some may need pieces with simpler ones.

HERE'S HOW TO CUSTOMIZE THE PATTERNS:

1. Choose your word families from the table of contents. Make a note of the page number.

2. Find the sorting piece with the matching page number and make copies. (You can cut out the pieces that go with your mat, and save the rest for later.)

3. Write any words you choose from the appropriate word family lists.

4. Add them to your sorting activity and you're ready to go!

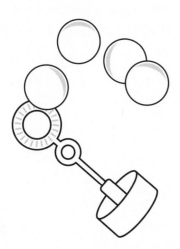

DIFFERENTIATION TIPS

Every teacher knows that one size does not fit all! Here are some tips for leveling the activities according to students' needs.

BEGINNING LEARNERS: Divide the activity into two parts: preparing and doing. Pair children up to cut out the pieces and color them with light shades of crayon. They can also color the mat. The next day, the pair can do the activity, and take turns writing the words on the practice sheet.

INTERMEDIATE LEARNERS: As children place each word, they can read the word quietly aloud. Have them use the writing practice sheet for self-assessment—they can focus primarily on words that gave them trouble.

ADVANCED LEARNERS: Create a challenge with a timer! See if children can sort all the words in a minute. They can also time how long it takes them to write all the words. Then they can write the words again, trying to beat their own time.

HELPFUL WORD LISTS

The patterns in this book contain words from 34 of the top word families. Here are additional words from each word family in this book.

Long and Short *a* Word Families										
-ail	**-ain**	**-ake**	**-ay**		**-ab**	**-ack**		**-ash**	**-at**
bail	main	fake	bay	gay	cab	hack	stack	bash	bat
fail	pain	make	hay	jay	dab	knack	track	cash	fat
hail	vain	quake	lay	may	jab	lack	whack	gash	gnat
jail	vain	rake	nay	pay	gab	quack		hash	pat
nail	brain	sake	ray	clay	lab	rack		lash	sat
quail	drain	take	fray	gray	nab	sack		sash	vat
rail	grain	wake	pray		blab	tack		brash	brat
sail	plain	brake	slay		drab	black		clash	chat
wail	slain	drake	spray		flab	clack		flash	flat
flail	sprain	flake	stay		scab	crack		slash	scat
frail	stain	shake	stray		slab	shack		smash	slat
trail	strain	stake	sway		stab	slack		stash	spat
			tray			smack		thrash	that

Long and Short *e* Word Families								
-eak	**-eed**	**-eat**	**-eep**	**-ed**	**-ell**	**-ent**	**-est**
peak	deed	feat	deep	led	cell	cent	jest
weak	heed	meat	jeep	wed	dell	dent	lest
bleak	reed	peat	peep	bled	fell	gent	pest
creak	bleed	bleat	seep	bred	jell	lent	vest
freak	breed	cheat	weep	fled	sell	rent	west
sneak	creed	cleat	cheep	shed	well	vent	zest
squeak	freed	pleat	creep	shred	dwell	scent	blest
streak	greed	wheat	steep	sped	shell	spent	chest
tweak	speed		sweep		spell		crest
	tweed				swell		quest
							wrest

Short *i* Word Families								
-ick	**-ill**		**-ing**		**-ink**	**-ip**		**-it**
quick	bill	dill	bing	ding	kink	dip	hip	hit
tick	gill	kill	ping	zing	link	lip	nip	knit
wick	mill	pill	bring	cling	mink	quip	tip	lit
brick	quill	sill	fling	sling	rink	blip	clip	pit
chick	till	chill	spring		wink	drip	flip	quit
click	drill	frill	sting		brink	grip	ship	wit
flick	grill	skill	string		clink	skip	slip	flit
slick	still	thrill	swing		shrink	snip	strip	grit
stick	trill	twill	thing		slink	trip	whip	skit
thick			wring		stink			slit
trick					think			spit
								split

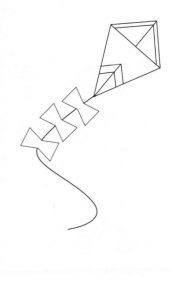

Long and Short *o* Word Families						Short *u* Word Families					
-one	**-ow**	**-ob**	**-ock**	**-op**	**-ot**	**-ub**	**-uck**	**-ug**	**-um**	**-ump**	**-unk**
hone	low	cob	dock	bop	cot	dub	buck	dug	bum	hump	bunk
lone	mow	gob	hock	cop	got	hub	muck	hug	mum	pump	hunk
tone	row	lob	knock	pop	jot	nub	puck	lug	sum	rump	drunk
zone	sow	mob	lock	sop	knot	sub	suck	mug	chum	chump	flunk
clone	tow	rob	mock	chop	lot	flub	tuck	pug	glum	clump	plunk
drone	blow	sob	tock	crop	rot	grub	cluck	chug	plum	frump	shrunk
prone	crow	blob	crock	drop	tot	scrub	pluck	drug	scum	grump	skunk
shone	flow	snob	flock	flop	blot	shrub	struck	plug	slum	plump	slunk
	glow	throb	shock	plop	clot	snub		shrug	strum	slump	spunk
	grow		smock	prop	plot	stub		slug	swum	stump	stunk
	show		stock	slop	shot			smug		thump	trunk
	slow			stop	slot			snug		trump	
	stow				spot			thug			
					trot						

MEETING THE STANDARDS

Read, Sort, and Write: Word Families is aligned with the Common Core State Standards in English Language Arts. See how this resource supports grade K–2 standards through the strands of foundational reading and writing skills.

READING: FOUNDATIONAL SKILLS

KINDERGARTEN

PRINT CONCEPTS:
RF.K.1 Demonstrate understanding of the organization and basic features of print.
RF.K.1.B Recognize that spoken words are represented in written language by specific sequences of letters.

PHONOLOGICAL AWARENESS:
RF.K.2 Demonstrate understanding of spoken words, syllables, and sounds (phonemes).
RF.K.2.A Recognize and produce rhyming words.
RF.K.2.C Blend and segment onsets and rimes of single-syllable spoken words.
RF.K.2.E Add or substitute individual sounds (phonemes) in simple, one-syllable words to make new words.

PHONICS AND WORD RECOGNITION:
RF.K.3 Know and apply grade-level phonics and word analysis skills in decoding words.

GRADE 1

PRINT CONCEPTS:
RF.1.1 Demonstrate understanding of the organization and basic features of print.
RF.1.3 Know and apply grade-level phonics and word analysis skills in decoding words.

PHONOLOGICAL AWARENESS:
RF.1.2 Demonstrate understanding of spoken words, syllables, and sounds (phonemes).

PHONICS AND WORD RECOGNITION:
RF.1.3.B Decode regularly spelled one-syllable words.

GRADE 2

PHONICS AND WORD RECOGNITION:
RF.2.3 Know and apply grade-level phonics and word analysis skills in decoding words.

LANGUAGE

KINDERGARTEN

CONVENTIONS OF STANDARD ENGLISH:
L.K.1.A Print many upper-and lowercase letters.
L.K.2 Demonstrate command of the conventions of standard English capitalization, punctuation, and spelling when writing.
L.K.2.C Write a letter or letters for most consonant and short-vowel sounds (phonemes).
L.K.2.D Spell simple words phonetically, drawing on knowledge of sound-letter relationships.

GRADE 1

CONVENTIONS OF STANDARD ENGLISH:
L.1.1.A Print all upper-and lowercase letters.
L.1.2 Demonstrate command of the conventions of standard English capitalization, punctuation, and spelling when writing.
L.1.2.D Use conventional spelling for words with common spelling patterns and for frequently occurring irregular words.

GRADE 2

CONVENTIONS OF STANDARD ENGLISH:
L.2.2 Demonstrate command of the conventions of standard English capitalization, punctuation, and spelling when writing.

WORD FAMILIES: -ail, -ain

Cut out the apples. Sort them into the baskets.

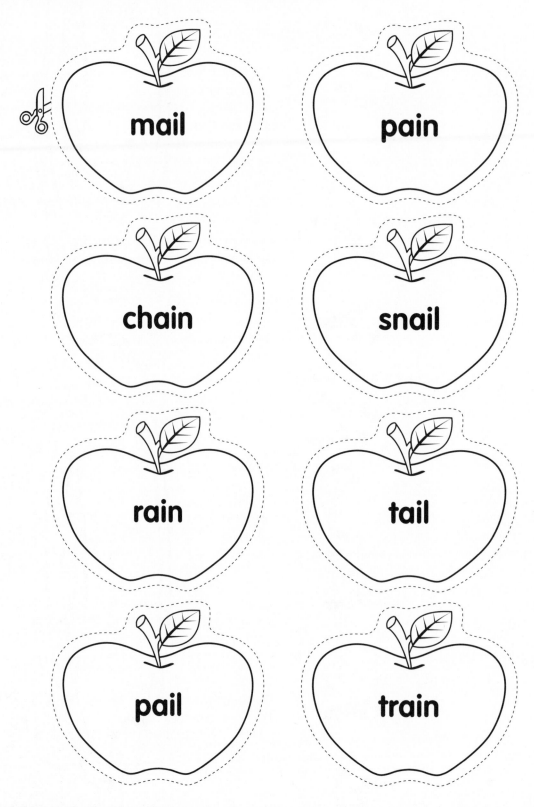

mail

pain

chain

snail

rain

tail

pail

train

Name: _____

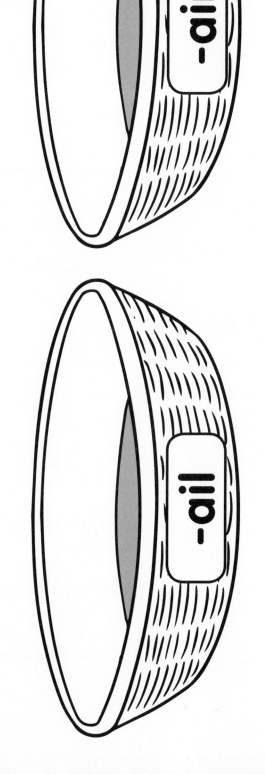

Name: _____

Trace then write each word.

-ail words

mail

pail

tail

snail

-ain words

pain

rain

chain

train

WORD FAMILIES: -ake, -ay

Cut out the pumpkins. Sort them onto the vines.

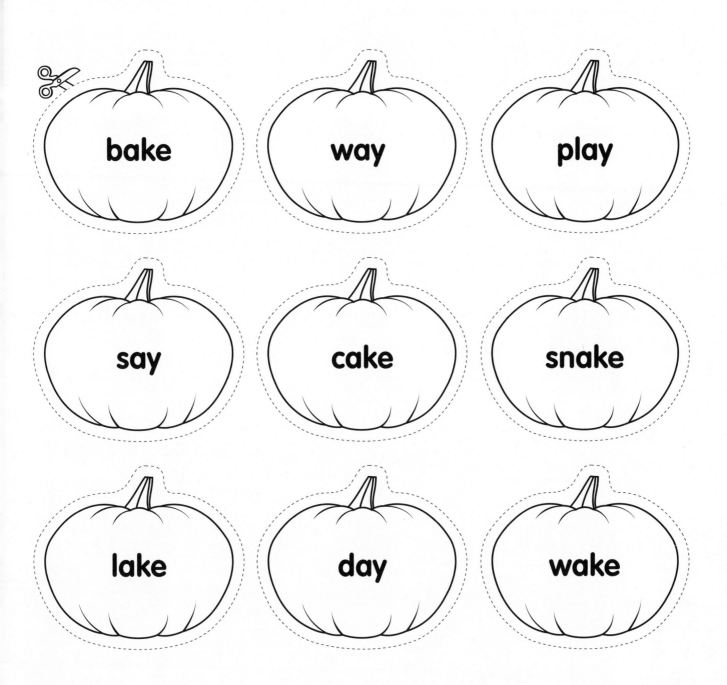

bake

way

play

say

cake

snake

lake

day

wake

Name: _____

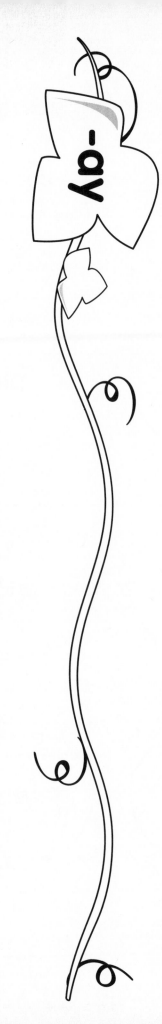

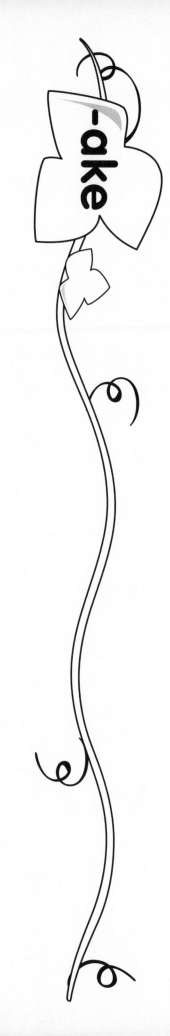

Name: _____

Trace then write each word.

-ake words

bake _____

cake _____

lake _____

snake _____

-ay words

day _____

say _____

way _____

play _____

WORD FAMILIES: -ab, -ack

Cut out the spiders. Sort them onto the webs.

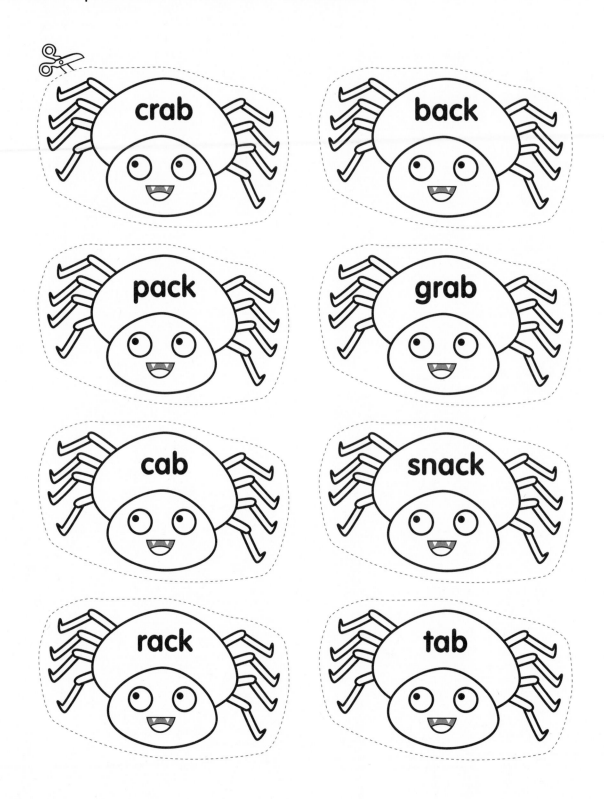

Name: _____

-ack

-ab

Name: _____

Trace then write each word.

-ab words

cab _____

tab _____

crab _____

grab _____

-ack words

back _____

pack _____

rack _____

snack _____

WORD FAMILIES: -ash, -at

Cut out the bats. Sort them into the caves.

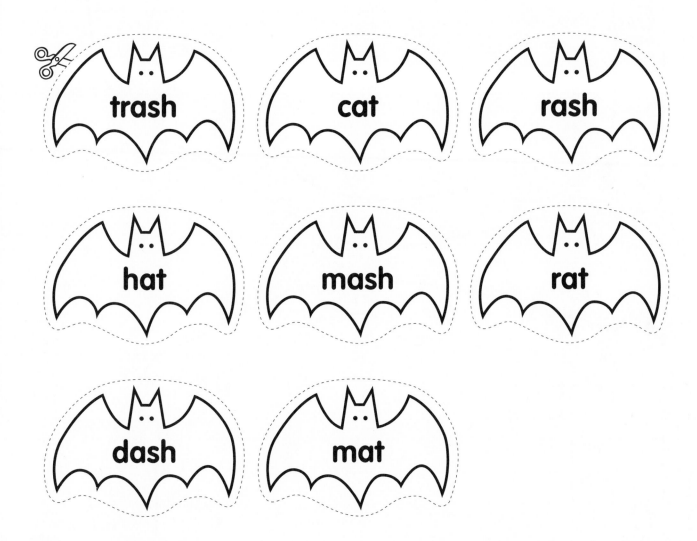

Name: _____

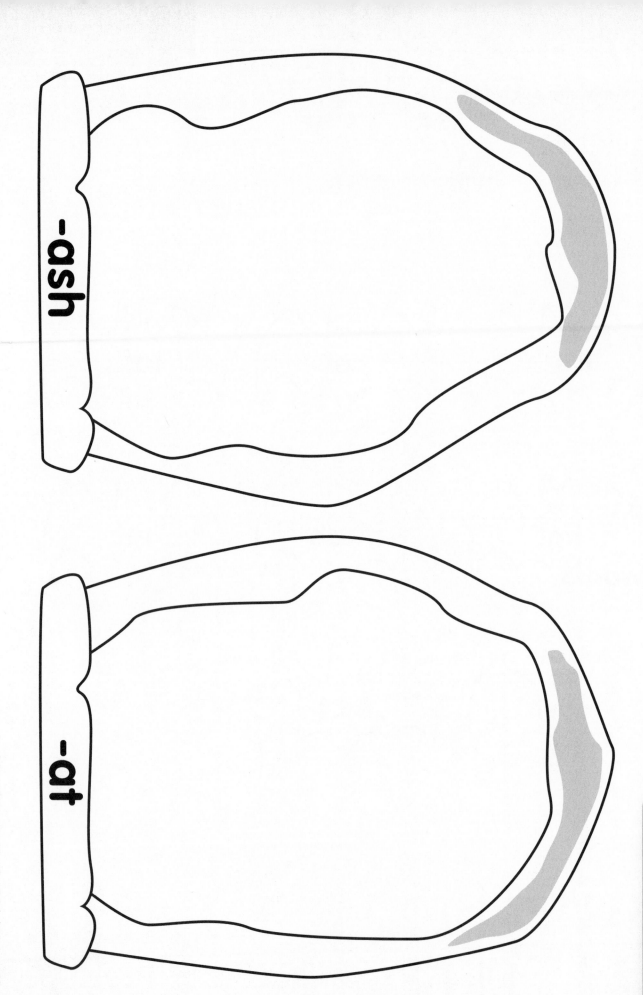

-ash

-at

Name: _____

Trace then write each word.

-ash words

dash _____

mash _____

rash _____

trash _____

-at words

cat _____

hat _____

mat _____

rat _____

WORD FAMILIES: -eak, -eed

Cut out the penguins. Sort them onto the ice floes.

beak

feed

leak

need

creak

seed

weed

speak

Name: _____

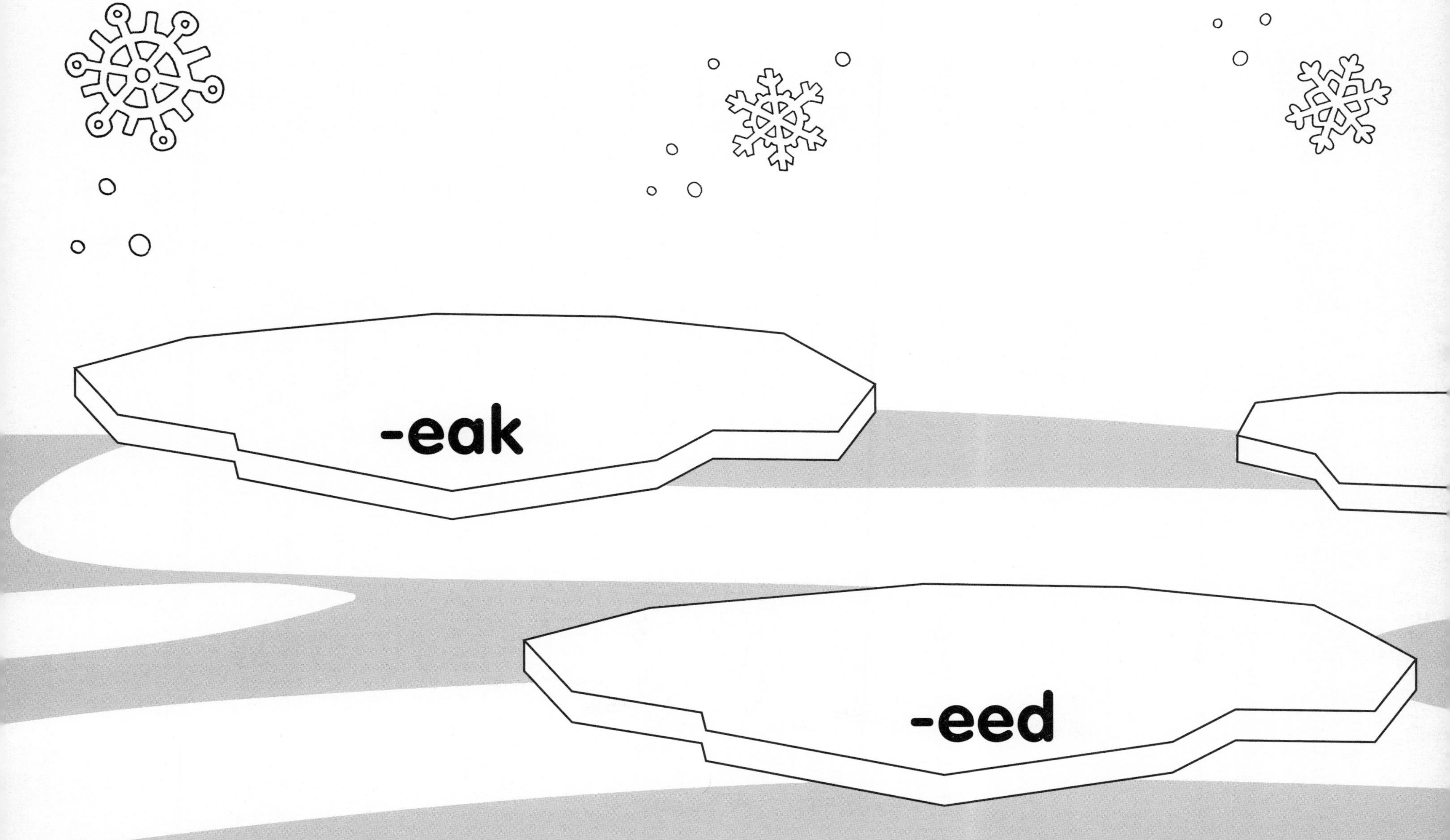

-eak

-eed

Name: _____

Trace then write each word.

-eak words

beak

leak

speak

creak

-eed words

feed

need

seed

weed

WORD FAMILIES: -eat, -eep

Cut out the bows. Sort them onto the presents.

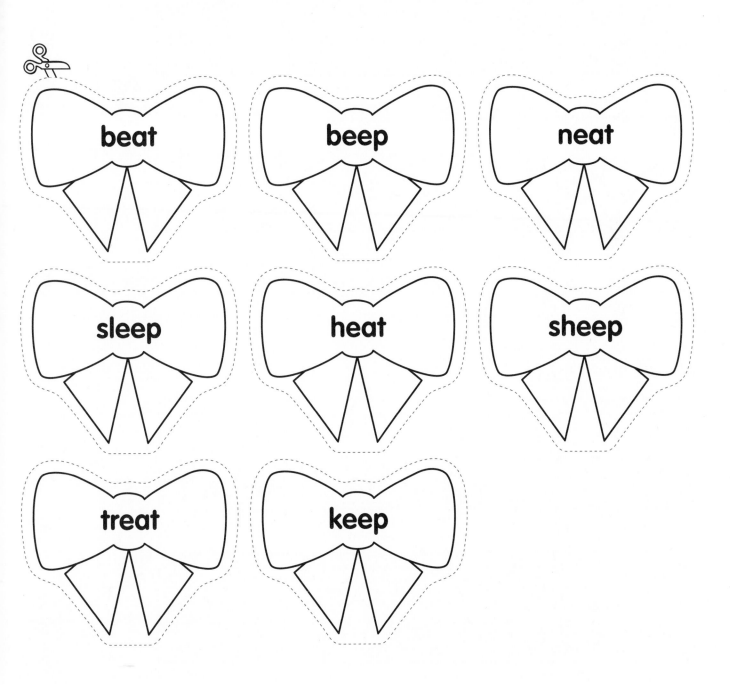

beat

beep

neat

sleep

heat

sheep

treat

keep

Name: _____

-eat

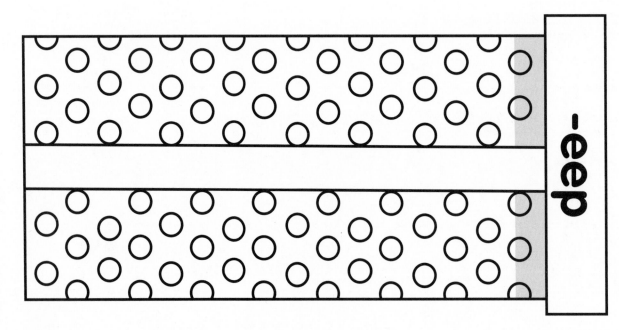

-eep

Name: _____

Trace then write each word.

-eat words

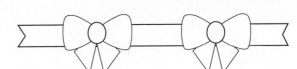

beat

heat

neat

treat

-eep words

beep

keep

sheep

sleep

WORD FAMILIES: -ed, -ell

Cut out the raindrops. Sort them under the rain cloud.

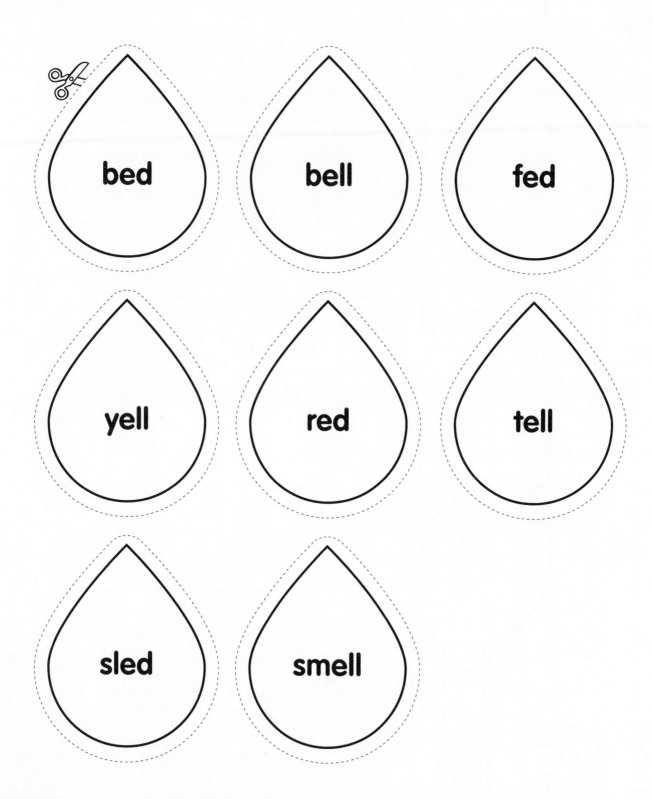

bed

bell

fed

yell

red

tell

sled

smell

Name: _____

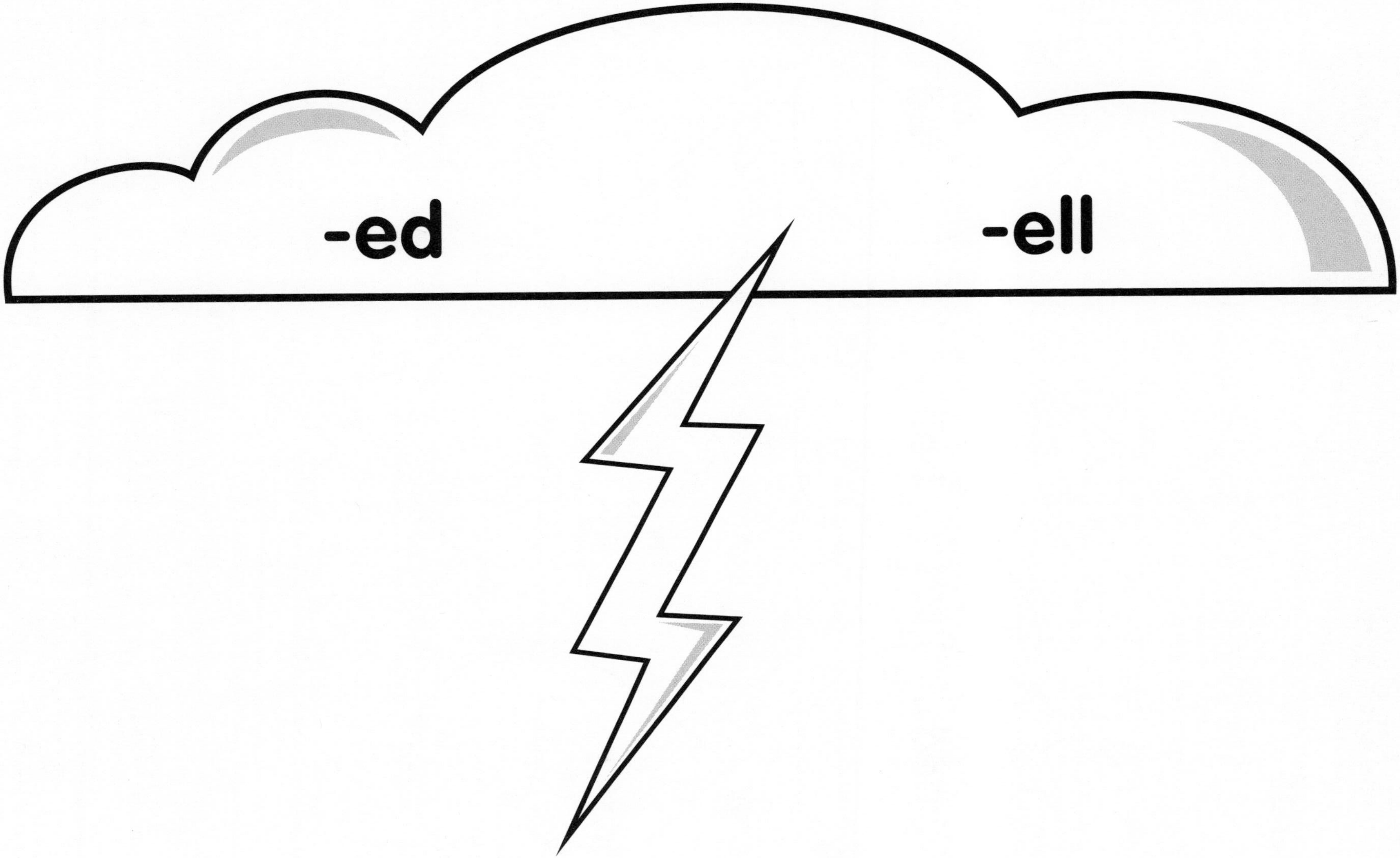

-ell

-ed

Name: _____

Trace then write each word.

-ed words

bed

fed

red

sled

-ell words

bell

yell

tell

smell

WORD FAMILIES: -ent, -est

Cut out the flowers. Sort them onto the stems.

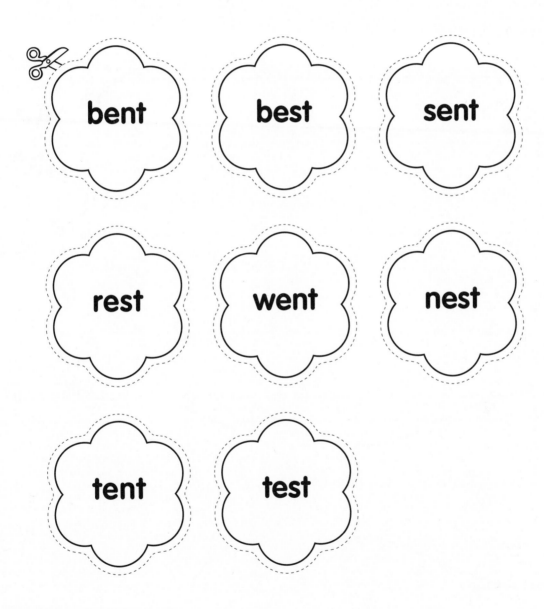

bent

best

sent

rest

went

nest

tent

test

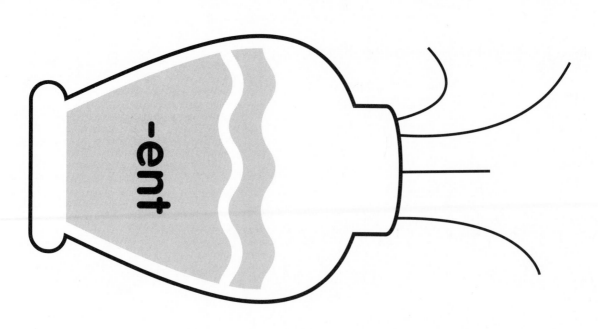

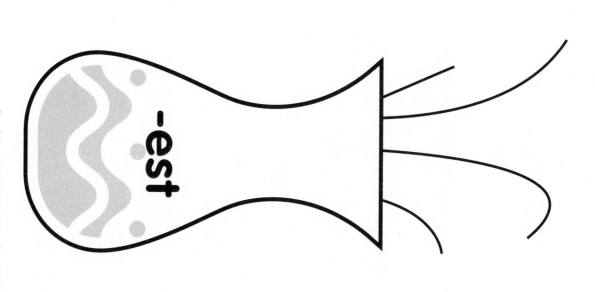

Name: _____

Trace then write each word.

-ent words

bent

sent

went

tent

-est words

best

nest

rest

test

WORD FAMILIES: -ick, -ill

Cut out the bows. Sort them onto the kite strings.

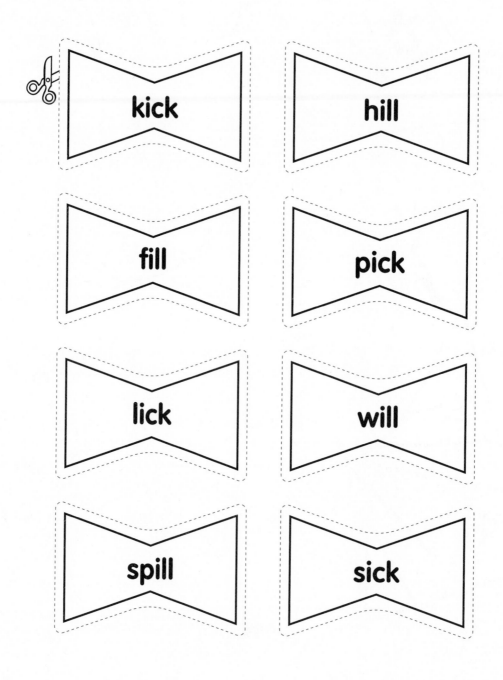

kick

hill

fill

pick

lick

will

spill

sick

Name: _____

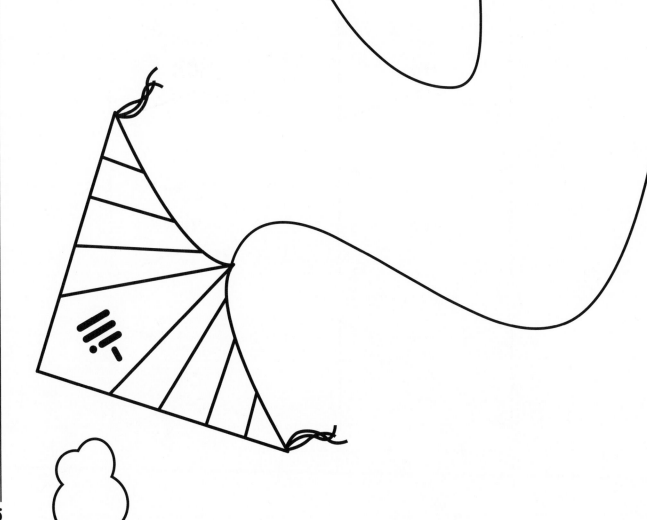

Name: _____

Trace then write each word.

-ick words

kick

pick

sick

lick

-ill words

hill

fill

will

spill

WORD FAMILIES: -ing, -ink

Cut out the bubbles. Sort them above the bubble wands.

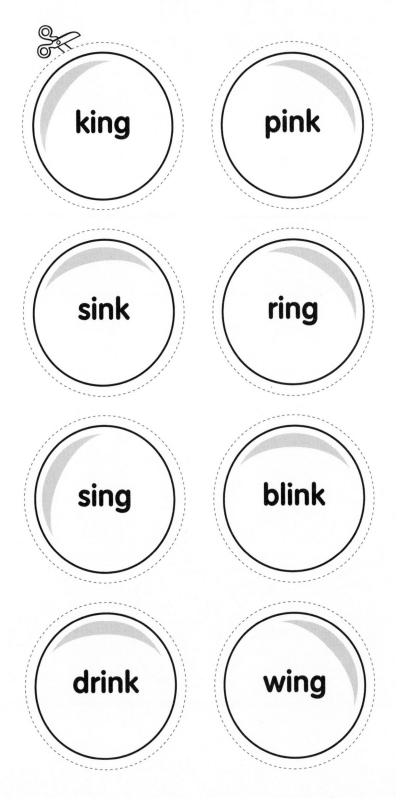

king

pink

sink

ring

sing

blink

drink

wing

Name: _____

Trace then write each word.

-ing words

king

ring

sing

wing

-ink words

pink

sink

blink

drink

WORD FAMILIES: -ip, -it

Cut out the chicks. Sort them under the hens.

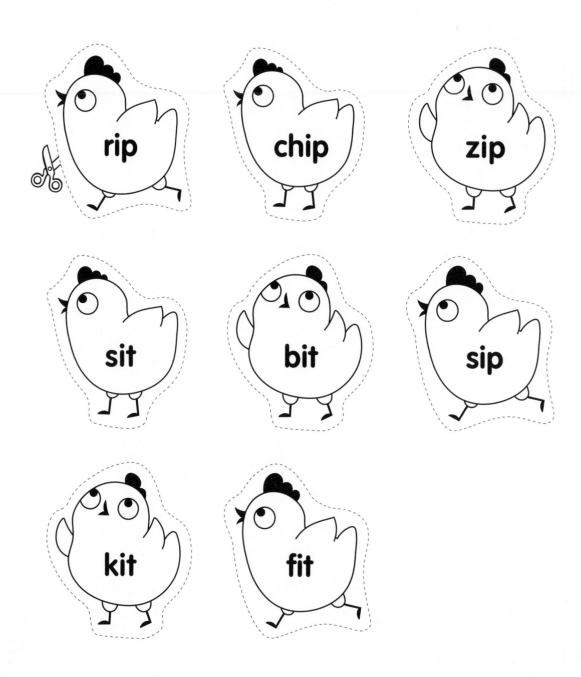

Name: _____

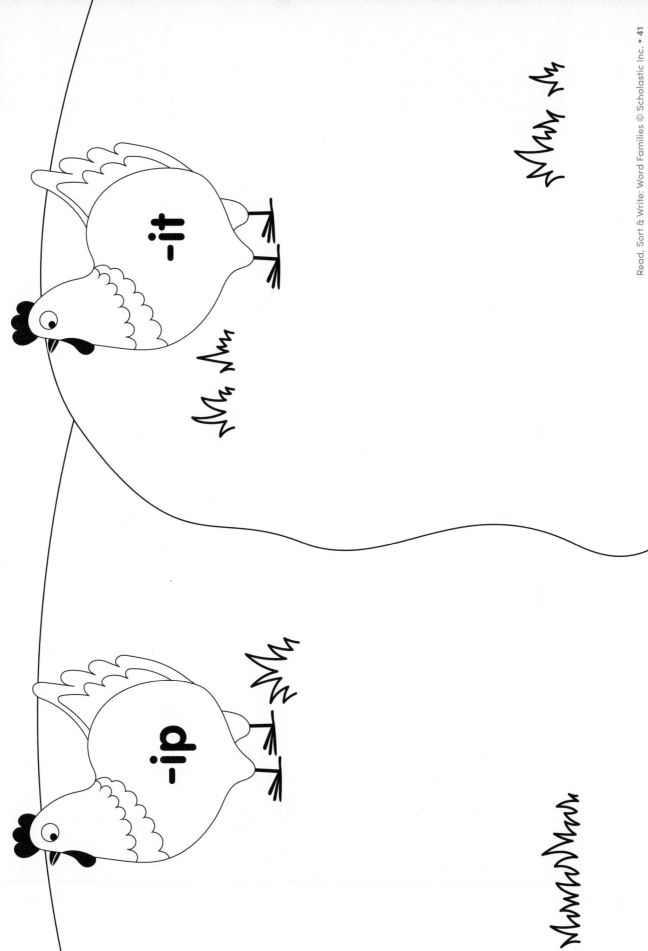

Name: _____

Trace then write each word.

-ip words

rip

sip

zip

chip

-it words

bit

fit

kit

sit

WORD FAMILIES: -one, -ow

Cut out the bugs. Sort them onto the leaves.

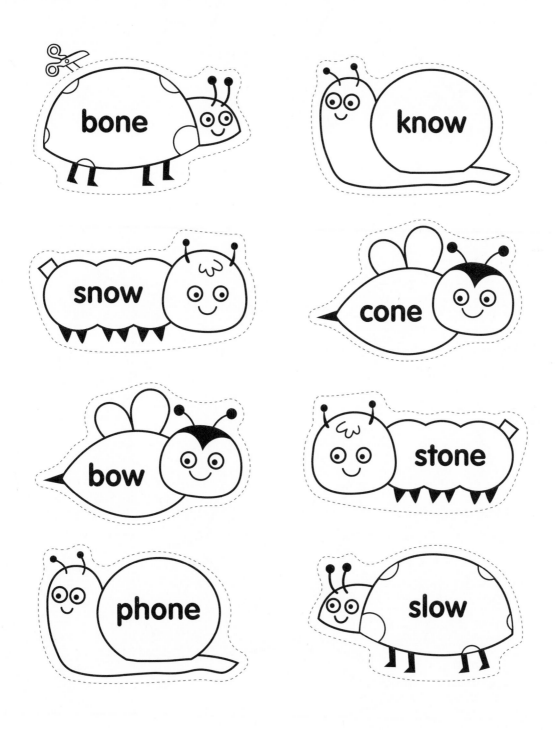

Name: _____

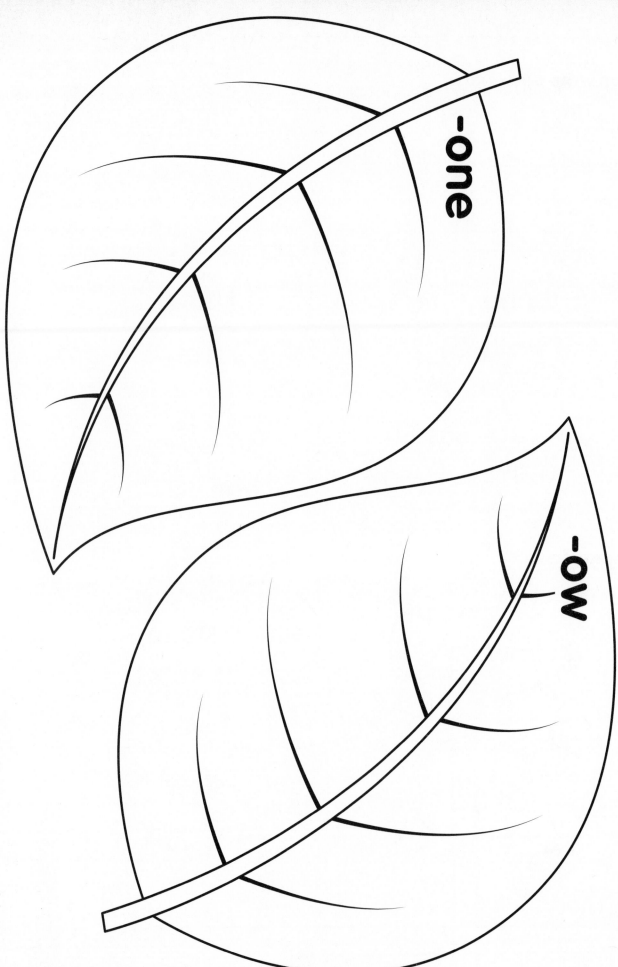

-one

-ow

WORD FAMILIES:
-one, -ow

Name: _____

Trace then write each word.

-one words

bone _____

cone _____

stone _____

phone _____

-ow words

bow _____

know _____

snow _____

slow _____

WORD FAMILIES: -ob, -ock

Cut out the fish. Sort them into the pond.

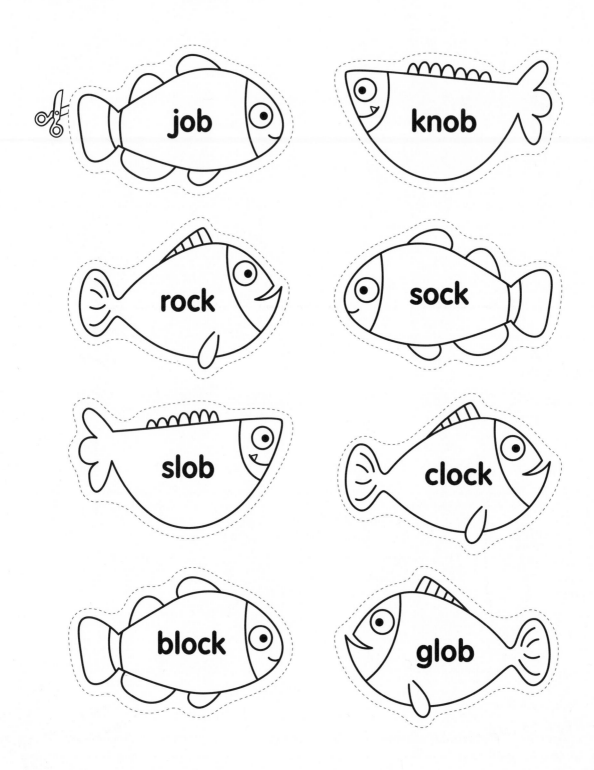

Name: _____

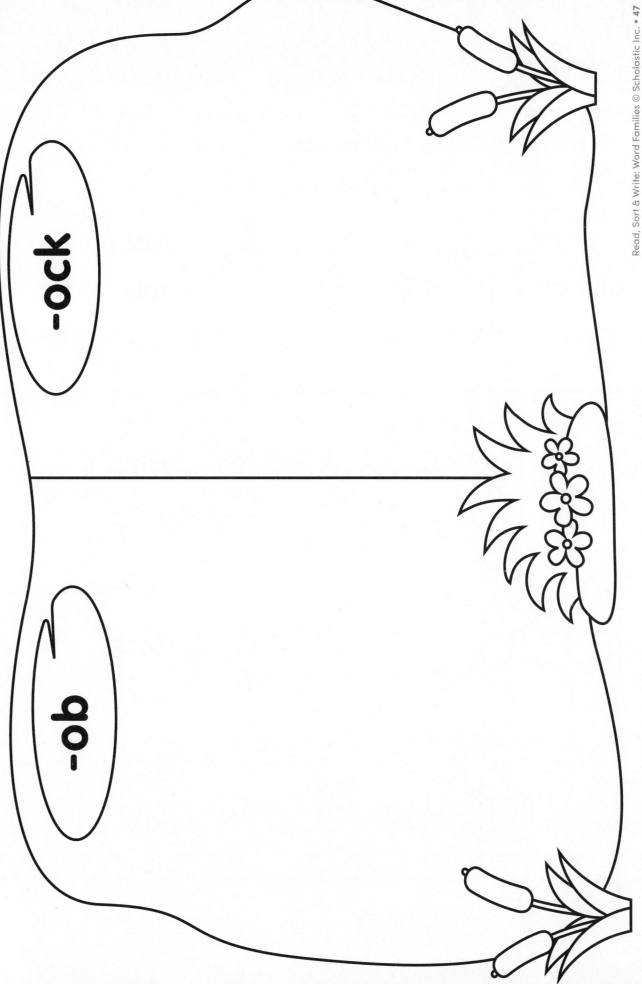

-ock

-ob

Name: _____

Trace then write each word.

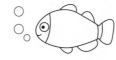  

-ob words

job

knob

slob

glob

-ock words

rock

sock

clock

block

WORD FAMILIES: -op, -ot

Cut out the seashells. Sort them onto the sand.

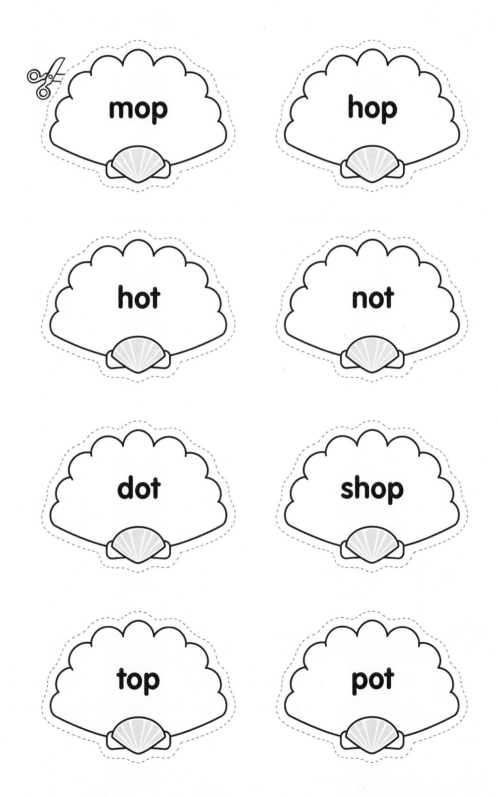

WORD FAMILIES:
-op, -ot

Name: _____

Trace then write each word.

-op words

hop

mop

top

shop

-ot words

dot

hot

not

pot

Cut out the ice cream scoops. Sort them into the cones.

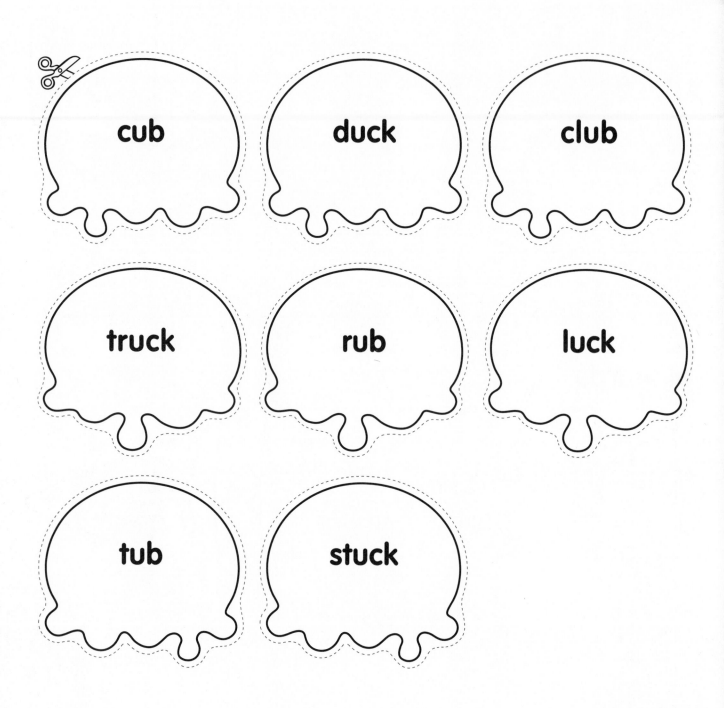

cub

duck

club

truck

rub

luck

tub

stuck

Name: _____

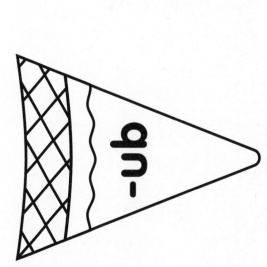

Name: _____

Trace then write each word.

-ub words

cub --

rub --

tub --

club ---------------------------------------

-uck words

duck ---------------------------------------

luck ---------------------------------------

truck --------------------------------------

stuck --------------------------------------

Cut out the balls. Stack them on top of the seals' noses.

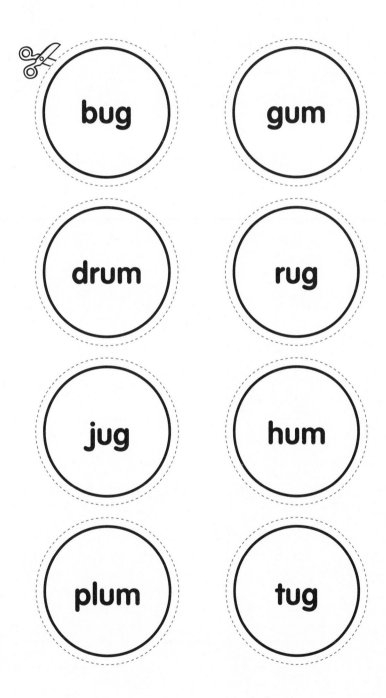

-ug

-um

Name: _____

Trace then write each word.

-ug words

bug _____

rug _____

jug _____

tug _____

-um words

gum _____

hum _____

drum _____

plum _____

WORD FAMILIES: -ump, -unk

Cut out the biscuits. Sort them into the dog bowls.

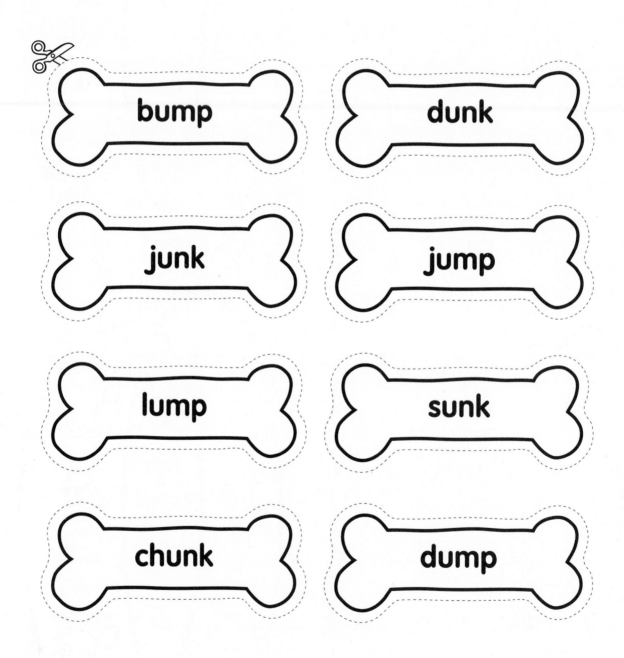

bump

dunk

junk

jump

lump

sunk

chunk

dump

Name: _____

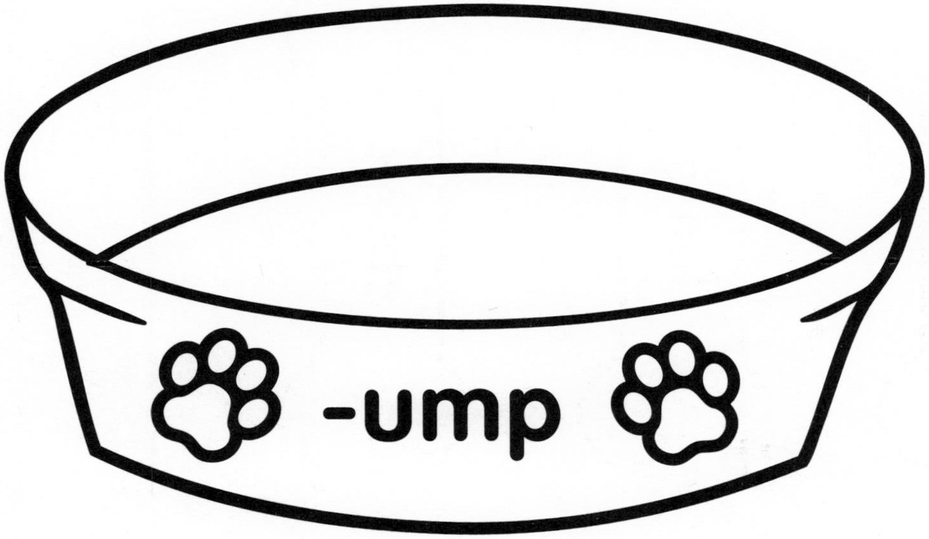

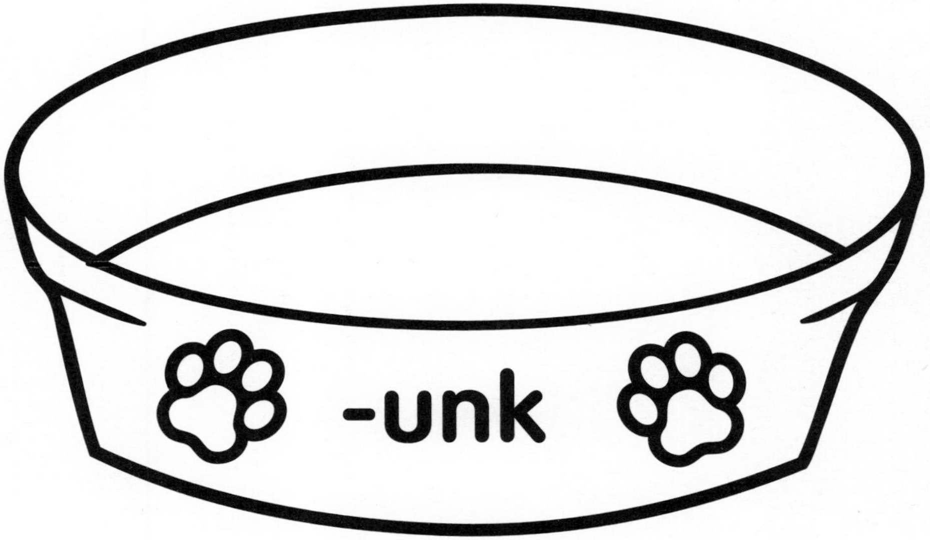

-unk

-ump

Name: _____

Trace then write each word.

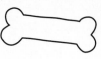

-ump words

bump

jump

lump

dump

-unk words

dunk

junk

sunk

chunk

Cut out the cookies. Sort them into the jars.

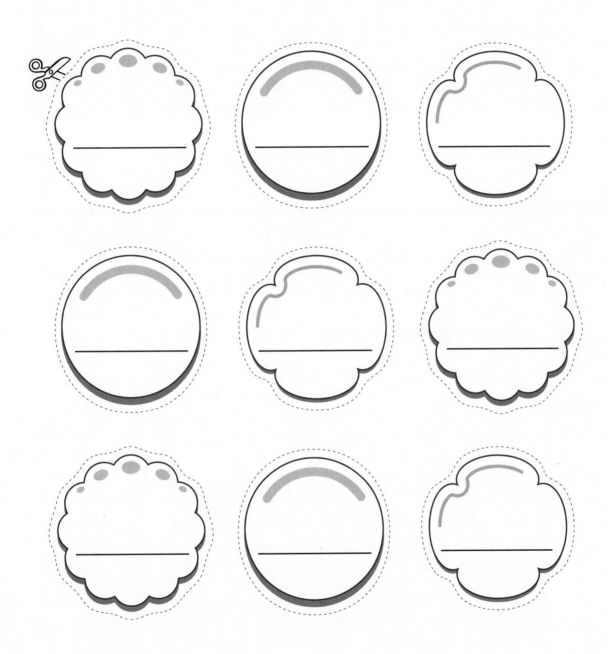

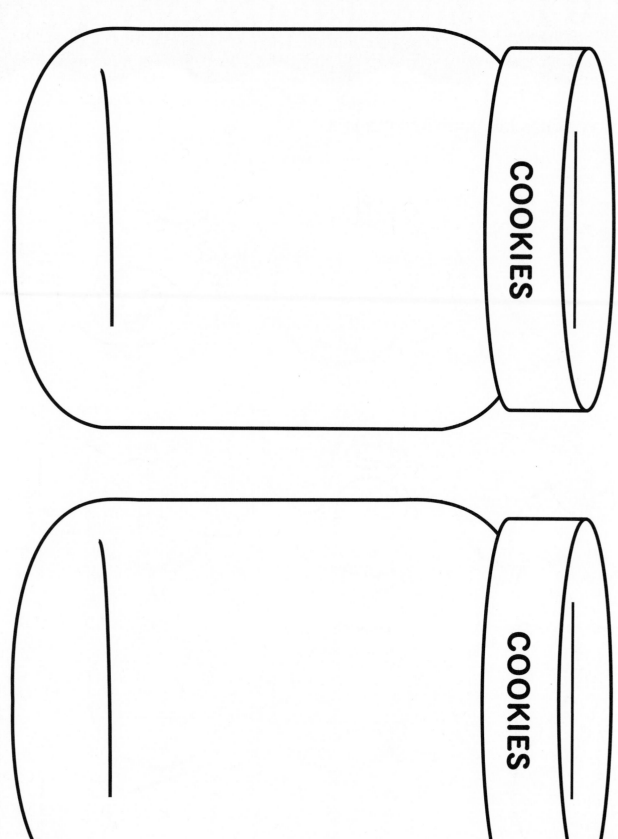

COOKIES

COOKIES

WORD FAMILIES:
Create Your Own

Blank Sorting Templates

Use these templates to customize your activities.

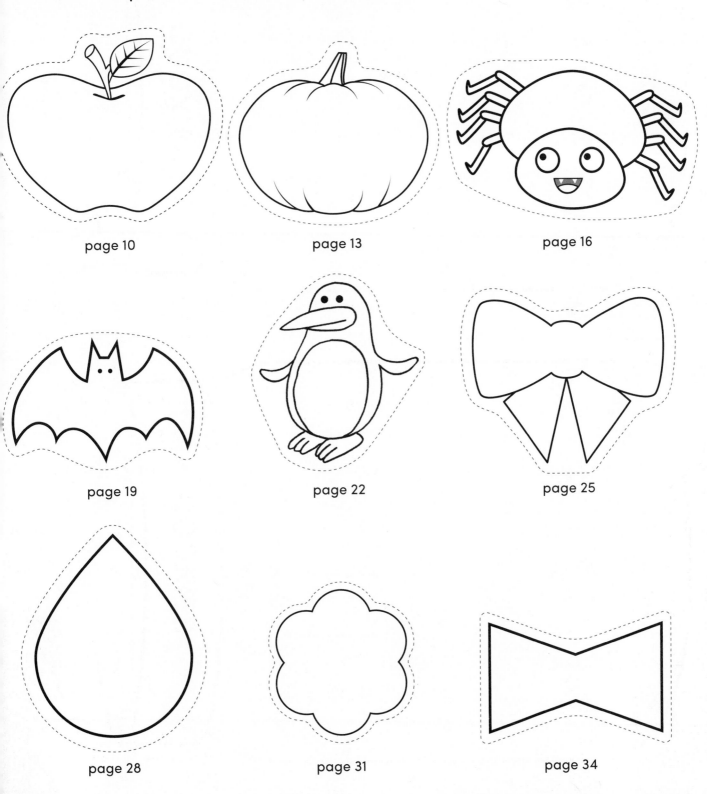

page 10

page 13

page 16

page 19

page 22

page 25

page 28

page 31

page 34

Blank Sorting Templates

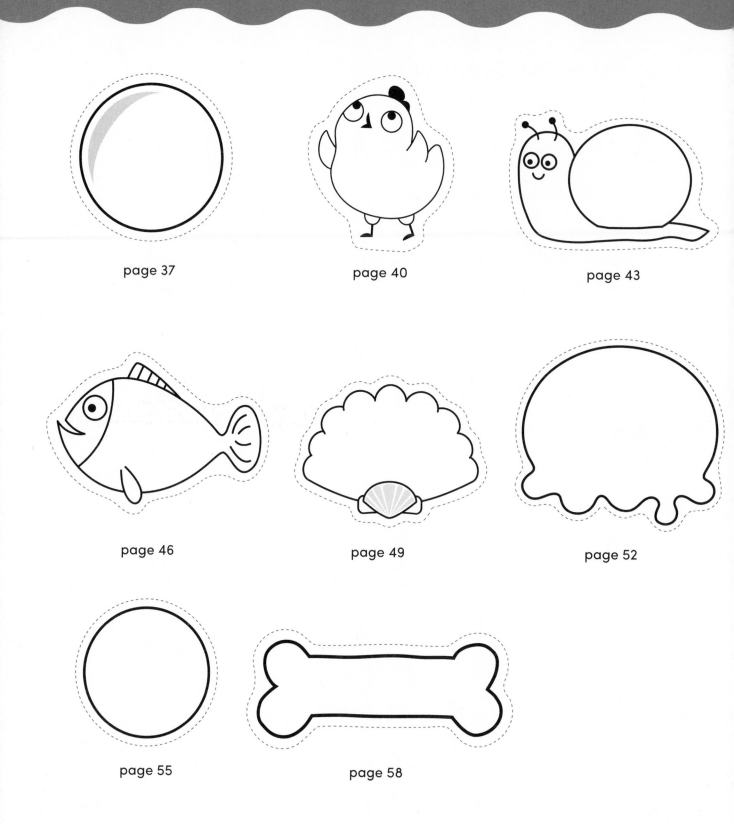

page 37

page 40

page 43

page 46

page 49

page 52

page 55

page 58